The Michael Jackson Collection

Project Manager: Sy Feldman
Art Layout: Deborah Johns

Cover Photography: Bill Nation
© 1995 Triumph Merchandising, Inc.
All rights reserved. Used by permission.

WARNER BROS. PUBLICATIONS - THE GLOBAL LEADER IN PRINT
USA: 15800 NW 48th Avenue, Miami, FL 33014

WARNER/CHAPPELL MUSIC
CANADA: 15800 N.W. 48th AVENUE
MIAMI, FLORIDA 33014
SCANDINAVIA: P.O. BOX 533, VENDEVAGEN 85 B
S-162 15, DANDERYD, SWEDEN
AUSTRALIA: P.O. BOX 353
3 TALAVERA ROAD, NORTH RYDE N.S.W. 2113
ASIA: UNIT 901 - LIPPO SUN PLAZA
28 CANTON ROAD
TSIM SHA TSUI, KOWLOON, HONG KONG

Carisch
NUOVA CARISCH
ITALY: VIA CAMPANIA, 12
20098 S. GIULIANO MILANESE (MI)
ZONA INDUSTRIALE SESTO ULTERIANO
SPAIN: MAGALLANES, 25
28015 MADRID
FRANCE: CARISCH MUSICOM,
25, RUE D'HAUTEVILLE, 75010 PARIS

IMP
INTERNATIONAL MUSIC PUBLICATIONS LIMITED
ENGLAND: GRIFFIN HOUSE,
161 HAMMERSMITH ROAD, LONDON W6 8BS
GERMANY: MARSTALLSTR. 8, D-80539 MUNCHEN
DENMARK: DANMUSIK, VOGNMAGERGADE 7
DK 1120 KOBENHAVNK

Contents

BEAT IT

Written and Composed by
MICHAEL JACKSON

Beat It - 3 - 1

2 BAD

Song and Lyrics Written by
MICHAEL JACKSON

Music Composed by
DALLAS AUSTIN, BRUCE SWEDIEN
and RENE MOORE

1. Told me that you're do - in' wrong.
3. Hell all up in Hol - ly - wood,

Word out shock - in' all a - lone.
say - in' that you got it good.

2 Bad - 7 - 1

12

THRILLER

Words and Music by
ROD TEMPERTON

Thriller - 6 - 1

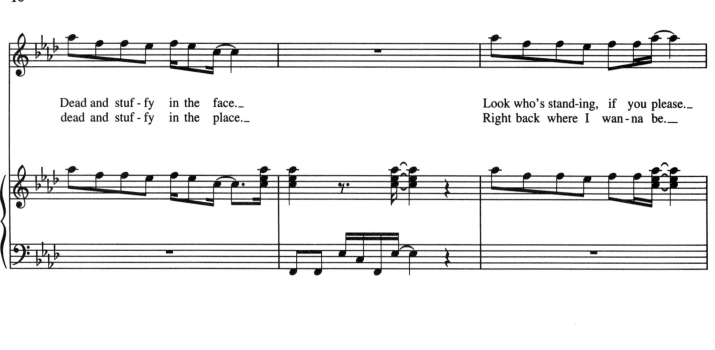

Dead and stuf - fy in the face._   Look who's stand-ing, if you please._
dead and stuf - fy in the place._   Right back where I wan-na be._

Though you tried to bring me to my knees._ }
I'm stand - in' though you're kick - in' me.__ }

Chorus:

Fm7   Bb/F

2 bad, 2 bad a-bout it,   why don't you scream and shout it?   2 bad, 2 bad a-bout it,

15

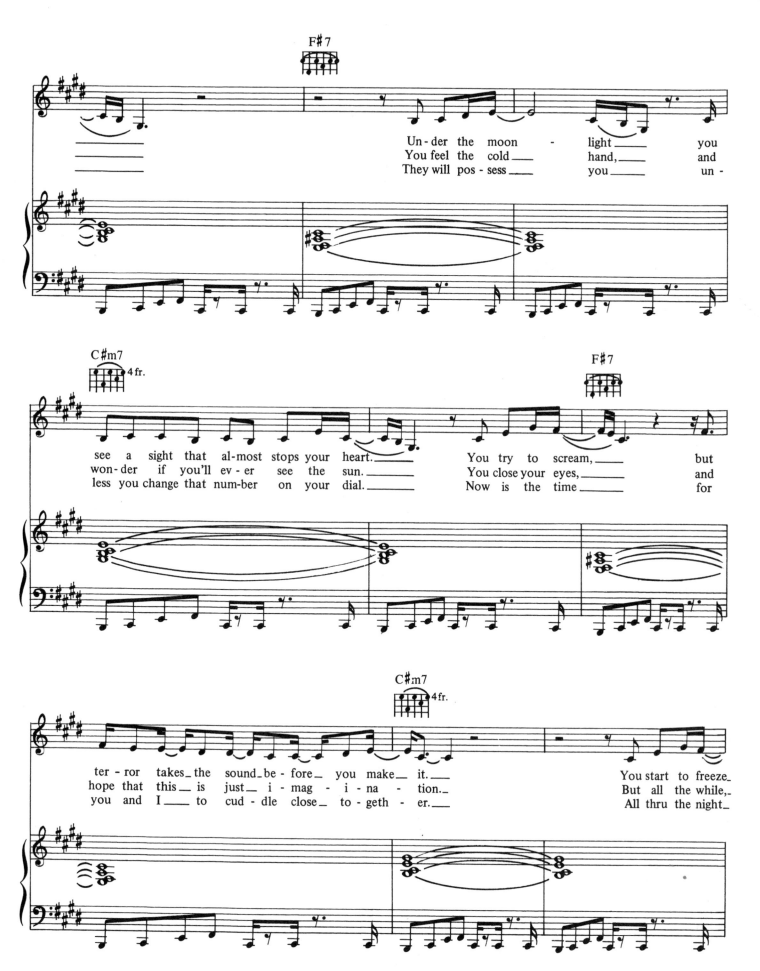

Thriller - 6 - 2

RAP: Darkness falls across the land.
        The midnight hour is close at hand.
        Creatures crawl in search of blood
        To terrorize y'awl's neighborhood.
        And whosoever shall be found
        Without the soul for getting down
        Must stand and face the hounds of hell
        And rot inside a corpse's shell.

        The foulest stench is in the air,
        The funk of forty thousand years,
        And grizzly ghouls from every tomb
        Are closing in to seal your doom.
        And though you fight to stay alive,
        Your body starts to shiver,
        For no mere mortal can resist
        The evil of a thriller.

SMOOTH CRIMINAL

Written and Composed by
MICHAEL JACKSON

Moderately

Smooth Criminal - 12 - 1

22

THE GIRL IS MINE

Written and Composed by
MICHAEL JACKSON

Ev-'ry night she walks_ right in _ my dreams, since I
un - der - stand_ the way_ you think, say - ing
build your hopes_ to be _ let down, 'cause I

The Girl Is Mine - 5 - 1

THEY DON'T CARE ABOUT US

Written and Composed by
MICHAEL JACKSON

1. Skin head, dead head, ev-ery-bod-y gone bad. Sit - u - a-tion, ag-grav-a-tion, ev-ery-bod-y al-leg-a-tion.
2. Beat me, hate me, you can nev-er break me. Will me, thrill me, you can nev-er kill me.
3. Skin head, dead head, ev-ery-bod-y gone bad. Trep-i - da-tion, spe-cu-la-tion, ev-ery-bod-y al-leg-a-tion.

In the suite, on the news ev-ery-bod - y dog food. Bang, bang, shock dead, ev-ery-bod-y's gone mad.
Chew me, sue me, ev-ery-bod - y do me. Kick me, hike me, don't you black or white me.
In the suite, on the news ev-ery-bod - y dog food. Black man, black-mail, throw the broth-er in jail.

All I wan-na say is that they don't real-ly care a - bout__ us.
All I wan-na say is that they don't real-ly care a - bout__ us.
All I wan-na say is that they don't real-ly care a - bout__ us.

They Don't Care About Us - 7 - 1

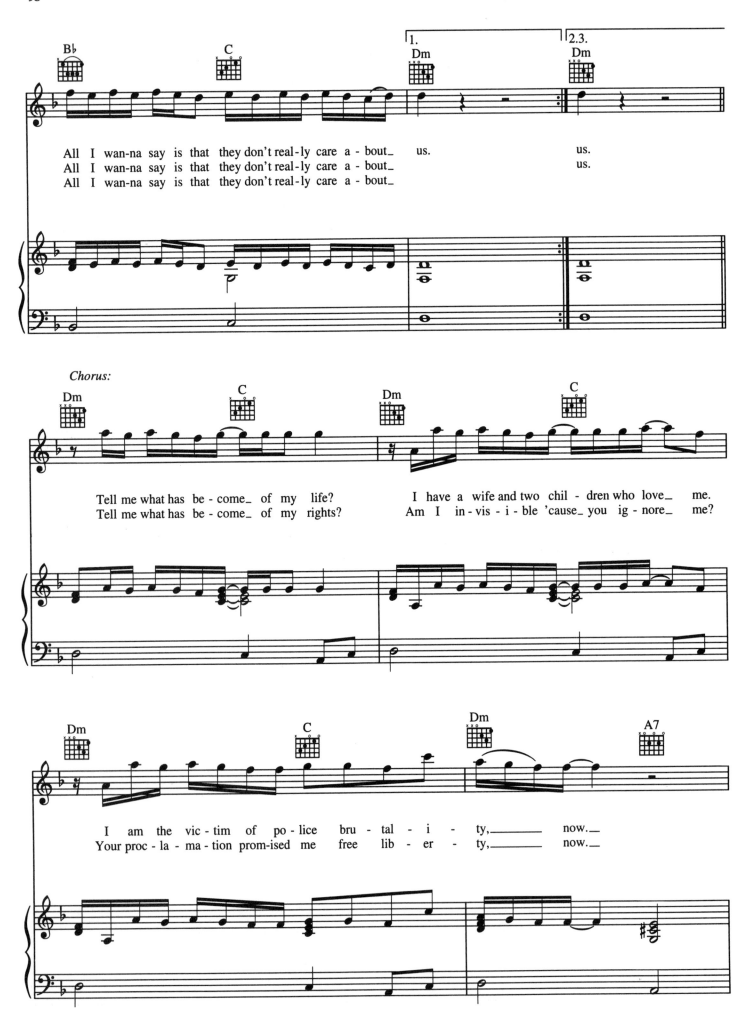

D.S. 𝄋 al Coda

⊕ *Coda*

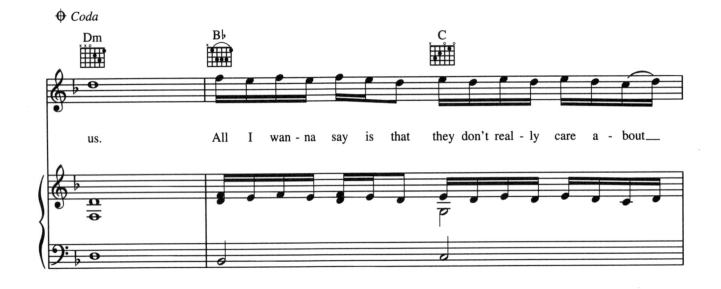

us.   All I wan-na say is that   they don't real-ly care a-bout___

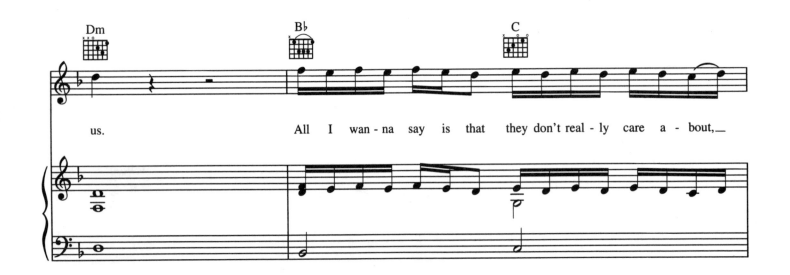

us.   All I wan-na say is that   they don't real-ly care a-bout,___

BILLIE JEAN

Written and Composed by
MICHAEL JACKSON

Billie Jean - 4 - 1

WILL YOU BE THERE
(from "Free Willy")

Written and Composed by
MICHAEL JACKSON

52

HEAL THE WORLD

PRELUDE BY MARTY PAICH

Written and Composed by
MICHAEL JACKSON

There's a place-

in your   heart-   and I   know---   that   it --- is   love.---   And this place.
to know   why-   there's a   love---   that   can - not   lie.---   Love is strong,-
so---   high,-   let our   spir - its   nev - er   die.---   In my   heart,-

58

YOU ARE NOT ALONE

Written and Composed by
R. KELLY

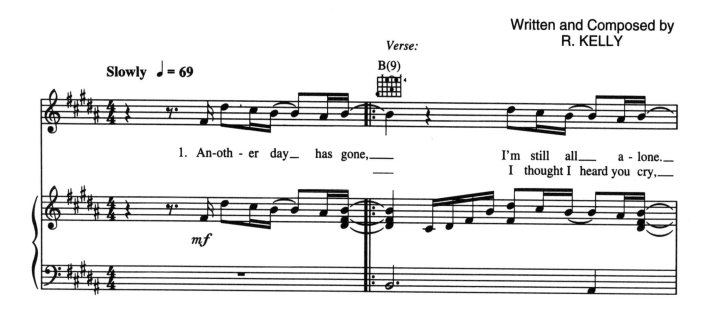

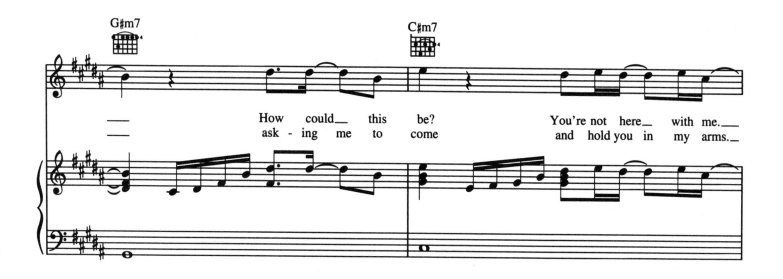

You Are Not Alone - 7 - 1

64

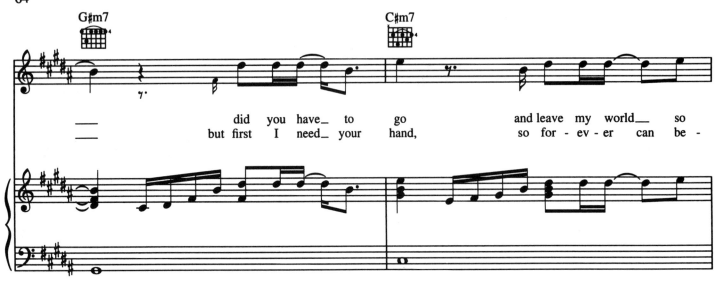

did you have_ to go ____ and leave my world_ so
but first I need_ your hand, ____ so for - ev - er can be-

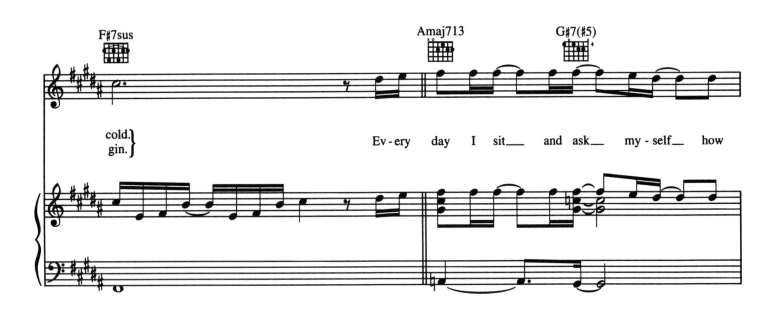

cold.}
gin.} Ev-ery day I sit_ and ask_ my-self_ how

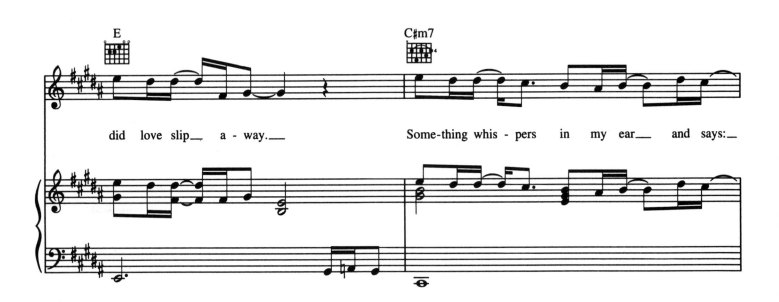

did love slip_ a - way._ Some-thing whis - pers in my ear_ and says:_

BAD

Written and Composed by
MICHAEL JACKSON

* These chords contain no 3rds.

Bad - 8 - 1

*Sing the lyrics between the asterisks 2nd time only.

N.C.

(Michael)

Am7 5fr. D9 4fr.

The word is out, you're
2. (Instrumental solo)

Am7 5fr. D9 4fr. Am7 5fr. D9 4fr.

do - in' wrong.— Gon - na lock you up _____ be - fore ___

Am7 5fr. D9 4fr. Am7 5fr. D9 4fr.

___ too long. Your ly - in' eyes gon - na

tell you right.____ So lis-ten up don't

1. make a fight.____ Your talk is cheap, you're

not a man.____ You're throw-in' stones, to hide____

____ your hands. But they _____ (End solo) We can

D.S. % al Coda ⊕

Bad - 8 - 6

Additional Lyrics
(For repeat)
You know I'm smooth-I'm
bad-you know it
(Bad bad-really, really bad)
You know I'm bad-I'm
bad baby
(Bad bad-really, really bad)
You know, you know, you
know it-come on
(Bad bad-really, really bad)
And the whole world has to
answer right now
(And the whole world has to
answer right now)
Woo!
(Just to tell you once again)

You know I'm bad, I'm bad-
you know it
(Bad bad-really, really bad)
You know I'm bad-you know-hoo!
(Bad bad-really, really bad)
You know I'm bad-I'm bad-
you know it, you know
(Bad bad-really, really bad)
And the whole world has to
answer right now
(And the whole world has to
answer right now)
Just to tell you once again...
(Just to tell you once
again...)
Who's bad?

SHE'S OUT OF MY LIFE

Written and Composed by
TOM BAHLER

She's Out of My Life - 4 - 4

MAN IN THE MIRROR

Words and Music by
SIEDAH GARRETT and GLEN BALLARD

Medium

I'm gon-na make a change,— for once in my _____ life.

It's gon-na feel ___ real ___ good,— gon-na make a diff-erence, gon-na make it right.—

Man in the Mirror - 13 - 1

86

90

Man in the Mirror - 13 - 10

Additional Lyrics for repeat:
(Yeah!-Make that change)
You know-I've got to get
    that man, that man...
(Man in the mirror)
You've got to
You've got to move! Come
    on! Come on!
You got to...
Stand up! Stand up!
    Stand up!
(Yeah!-Make that change)
Stand up and lift
    yourself, now!
(Man in the mirror)
Hoo! Hoo! Hoo!
Aaow!
(Yeah!-Make that change)
Gonna make that change...
    come on!
You know it!
You know it!
You know it!
You know...
(Change...)
Make that change.

THE WAY YOU MAKE ME FEEL

Medium Rock

Written and Composed by
MICHAEL JACKSON

Hee - hee!   Ooh! _____   Go on

girl!   Aaow!

The Way You Make Me Feel - 9 - 1

The Way You Make Me Feel - 9 - 3

Additional Lyrics for repeat:
Ain't nobody's business.
  ain't nobody's business
(The way you make me feel)
Ain't nobody's business.
Ain't nobody's business but
  mine and my baby
(You really turn me on)
Hee hee!
(You knock me off of
  my feet)
Hee hee! Ooh!
(My lonely days are gone)
Give it to me-give me
  some time
(The way you make me feel)
Come on be my girl-I wanna
  be with mine
(You really turn me on)
Ain't nobody's business-

(You knock me off of
  my feet)
Ain't nobody's business but
  mine and my baby's
Go on girl! Aaow!
(My lonely days are gone)
Hee hee! Aaow!
Chika-chika
Chika-chika-chika
Go on girl-Hee hee!
(The way you make me feel)
Hee hee hee!
(You really turn me on)
(You knock me off my feet)
(My lonely days are gone)
(The way you make me feel)
(You really turn me on)
(You knock me off my feet)
(My lonely days are gone)

DON'T STOP 'TIL YOU GET ENOUGH

Written and Composed by
MICHAEL JACKSON

106

SAY SAY SAY

Words and Music by
MICHAEL JACKSON and
PAUL McCARTNEY

Say, say,— say —— what you want but don't play—— games
Go, go,— go —— where you want but don't leave —— me
You, you,— you —— can nev-er say that I'm not — the one

with my af-fec-ion. Take, take,— take —— what you need but
here for-ev-er. You, you,— you —— stay a-way, so
who real-ly loves you. I pray, pray,— pray —— ev'ry day that

E♭m7 · B♭m · E♭m

don't leave ___ me ___ with no di - rect - ion. All a - lone ___ I sit home
long, girl ___ I ___ see you nev - er. What can I do ___ girl, to get
you'll see ___ things ___ girl, like I ___ do. What can I do ___ girl, to get

G♭ · B♭m

by the phone ___ wait - ing for ___ you ba - by.
through to you? ___ 'Cause I love ___ you ba - by.
through to you? ___ 'Cause I love ___ you ba - by.

E♭m · G♭ · F-10

Through the years ___ how can you stand to hear my plead - ing for you dear? You know I'm crying
Stand - ing here ___ bap - tised in all my tears, ba - by through the years, you know I'm crying}
Stand - ing here ___ bap - tised in all my tears, ba - by through the years, you know I'm crying}

To Coda ⊕
1
B♭m · B♭m7 · E♭ · E♭m7 · B♭m

ooh ooh ooh ooh ooh.

(Now)

Say Say Say - 4 - 2

BLACK OR WHITE

Written and Composed by
MICHAEL JACKSON

I took my ba - by on a Sat - ur - day bang.___
They print my mes - sage in the Sat - ur - day Sun.___

Boy, is that girl with you? Yes, we're one and the same.___ Now,
I had to tell them I ain't sec - ond to none.___ And I

Black or White - 6 - 4

121

IN THE CLOSET

Written and Composed by
MICHAEL JACKSON and TEDDY RILEY

Slowly and freely

(Whispered): There's something I have to say to you, if you promise you'll understand.

I cannot contain myself when in your presence. I'm so humble, just touch me.

Don't hide our love, woman to man.

Moderate Funk
No Chord

In the Closet - 8 - 1

124

In the Closet - 8 - 3

HISTORY

Written and Composed by
MICHAEL JACKSON,
JAMES HARRIS III and TERRY LEWIS

History - 7 - 1

How man-y vic - tims must there_ be__ slaught - ered in vain___ a-cross the land?__
How man-y peo - ple have to__ cry_ the song of pain and grief___ a-cross the land?__

— And how man-y strug - gles must there be_____ be -
— And how man-y child - ren have to die____ be -

fore we choose to live the proph - et's plan?
fore we stand to lend a heal - ing hand?   Ev - 'ry-bod - y sing:

Chorus:

Ev-'ry day_ cre-ate your his-to-ry._ Ev-'ry path_ you take, you're

leav - ing_ your leg - a - cy. Ev-'ry sol - dier dies in his glo-ry._

Ev-'ry leg - end tells of con - quest_ and lib-er - ty._

SCREAM

Written and Composed by
MICHAEL JACKSON, JANET JACKSON,
JAMES HARRIS III and TERRY LEWIS

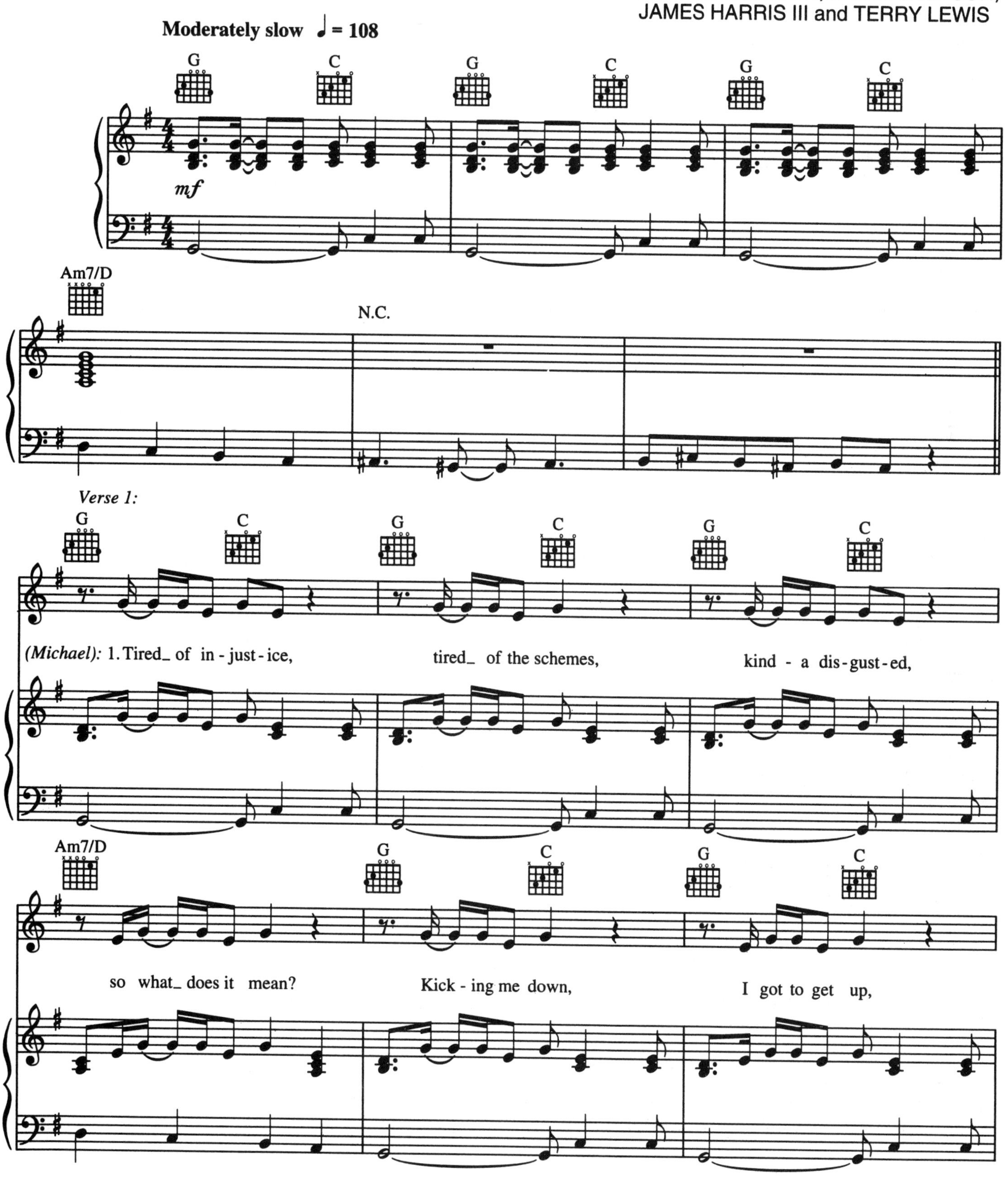

Moderately slow ♩ = 108

Verse 1:

(Michael): 1. Tired of in-just-ice, tired of the schemes, kind-a dis-gust-ed,

so what does it mean? Kick-ing me down, I got to get up,

Scream - 7 - 1

just can't take it.

ROCK WITH YOU

Words and Music by
ROD TEMPERTON

GHOSTS

Moderately slow ♩ = 96

Written and Composed by
MICHAEL JACKSON and TEDDY RILEY

Verse:

1. There's a ghost out in the hall,_ there's a
(2. 3.) thump-ing in the floor,_ there's a

ghoul up un - der the bed._ There's some-thing in the walls,_ there's blood up-on_ the stairs._ And there's
creak be-hind_ the door. There's a rock-ing in the chair,_ but there's no one sit - ting there._ There's a

groan-ing through_ the room,_ and there's noth-ing I___can see._ And I know this place_ is a tomb,_ be-cause
ghost-ly smell_ a - round,_ but no - bod - y to_ be found._ And the cof - fin lay_ o - pen_ where a

BLOOD ON THE DANCE FLOOR

Written and Composed by
MICHAEL JACKSON and
TEDDY RILEY

Moderately slow ♩ = 92

Blood on the Dance Floor - 6 - 1

Verse:

N.C.

1. She got your num - ber,__ she know your game. She put you un - der,__
2. She got your num - ber.__ How does it feel to know the stran - ger__

it's so in - sane. Since she se - duced you,__ how does it feel
is out to kill? She got your ba - by,__ it hap - pened fast.

to know that wom - an__ is out to kill? }
If you could on - ly__ e - rase the past. } Ev -

'ry night stance is like tak-in' a chance._It's not__ a - bout love and ro - mance,_ and now_ you're gon - na

get it.

Ev - 'ry hot man is out tak-in' a chance._ It's not_ _ a-bout love and ro - mance,_ and now_ you do re - gret it.

Bridge:

To es-cape_ the world,_ I've got_ to en - joy {that / this} sim - ple dance._ And it seemed_

_ that ev - 'ry-thing_was on_ my side._ (Blood on my side.) It seemed_to me_ like it_ was love._

158

Blood on the Dance Floor - 6 - 5

Repeat ad lib. and fade

EARTH SONG

Written and Composed by
MICHAEL JACKSON

162

164

Verse 2:
What about animals?
  (What about it?)
We've turned kingdoms to dust?
  (What about us?)*
What about elephants?
Have we lost their trust?
What about crying whales?
We're ravaging the seas.
What about forest trails,
  (Ooh, ooh.)
Burnt despite our pleas?

Verse 3:
What about the holy land
  (What about it?)
Torn apart by creed?
What about the common man,
Can't we set him free?
What about children dying?
Can't you hear them cry?
Where did we go wrong?
  (Ooh, ooh.)
Someone tell me why.

Verse 4:
What about babies
  (What about it?)
What about the days?
What about all their joy?
What about the man?
What about the crying man?
What about Abraham?
What about death again?
  (Ooh, ooh.)
Do we give a damn?
(To Chorus:)

*Repeat after every line except where specified.

CHILDHOOD

Slowly, with expression (♩ = 90)

Written and Composed by
MICHAEL JACKSON

Have you seen my Child - hood? I'm search-ing for the world that I___ come from. 'Cause I've_ been look-ing a-round___ in the lost and found___ of my heart. No one un-der- stands me, they view it as such strange ec-cen-tric-i-ties.___

hard to love me, look with-in your heart then ask,___

have you seen my Child-hood?

DIRTY DIANA

Written and Composed by
MICHAEL JACKSON

* Sing the lyrics, "Dirty Diana, nah." twice, last time only.

Dirty Diana - 6 - 4

Dirty Diana - 6 - 6

I JUST CAN'T STOP LOVING YOU

Written and Composed by
MICHAEL JACKSON

Spoken: I just want to lay next to you for awhile.

Freely

You look so beautiful tonight. Your eyes are so lovely, your mouth is so sweet.

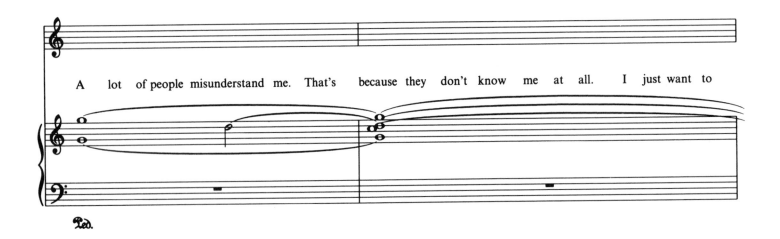

A lot of people misunderstand me. That's because they don't know me at all. I just want to

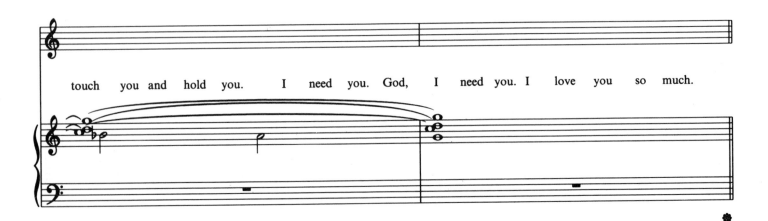

touch you and hold you. I need you. God, I need you. I love you so much.

I Just Can't Stop Loving You - 7 - 1

Sung: *(Michael)*

Each time the wind ____ blows, I hear your voice, ____ so

I call your name.

Whis-pers at morn - ing,

our love is dawn - ing, heav-en's glad ____ you came. ____

I Just Can't Stop Loving You - 7 - 4

182

I Just Can't Stop Loving You - 7 - 5

I Just Can't Stop Loving You - 7 - 6

Additional Lyrics (for Repeat and Fade)

(Both): I just can't stop loving you.
(Michael): Hee! Hee! Hee! Know I do, girl.
(Both): I just can't stop loving you.
(Michael): You know I do. And if I stop,
(Both): Then tell me just what will I do?

HUMAN NATURE

Words and Music by
JOHN BETTIS and STEVE PORCARO

Look - ing___ out ___ a - cross_ the night -

Human Nature - 7 - 1

Human Nature - 7 - 3

188

Human Nature - 7 - 5

Human Nature - 7 - 7

REMEMBER THE TIME

Written and Composed by MICHAEL JACKSON,
BERNARD BELLE and TEDDY RILEY

Moderately

Do you re - mem-

Remember the Time - 5 - 1

194

Additional Lyrics

Do you remember the time
When we fell in love
Do you remember the time
When we first met
Do you remember the time
When we fell in love
Do you remember the time

Do you remember the time
When we fell in love
Do you remember the time
When we first met
Do you remember the time
When we fell in love
Do you remember the time

Remember the times
Ooh
Remember the times
Do you remember girl
Remember the times
On the phone you and me
Remember the times
Till dawn, two or three
What about us girl

Remember the times
Do you, do you, do you,
Do you, do you
Remember the times
In the park, on the beach
Remember the times
You and me in Spain
Remember the times
What about, what about...

Remember the times
Ooh... in the park
Remember the times
After dark... do you, do you, do you
Remember the times
Do you, do you, do you, do you
Remember the times
Yeah yeah

WANNA BE STARTIN' SOMETHIN'

Written and Composed by
MICHAEL JACKSON

Moderately bright

I said you wan-na be start-in' some-thin', you got ___ to be start-in' some-thin'. I said you

wan-na be start-in' some-thin', you got ___ to be start-in' some-thin'. It's too high ___

Wanna Be Startin' Somethin' - 7 - 1

200

Wanna Be Startin' Somethin' - 7 - 7